Q Me In

Marquita Ricketts

Presentation by *BookLeaf Publishing*

Web: www.bookleafpub.com

E-mail: info@bookleafpub.com

ISBN: 9789358312942

First edition 2023

My gratitude goes to God. Thank you for this moment and thank you for always keeping my Faith stronger than my sight.

My appreciation and adoration go to M, N, and E for still believing in me. Thank you for being the amazing people that you are and giving me life, daily. You all make every day an adventure-- one I would gladly continue, with you, forever. Thank you for being here.

To end:

Dedication goes to my readers, family and friends alike, and anyone else seeking a little light-- while picking flowers.

ACKNOWLEDGEMENT

To Life,

Thank you for all that you are and never portraying yourself as something you are not. I would like to think I have had many experiences with you, yet still have so much to learn from you.

PREFACE

This book and I are here because promises of writing more books were made– ironically, a good portion of this book is about choices. Most importantly, I am here because of this book. The journey has been long and tiring but "Q Me In" is and has been, a necessary experience. One to help me-- Understand. Forgive. Grow. Release. Be.

I needed to know

ME.

Day 1: Sticks, Stones, and Bridges

My past taught me.
I fought long and hard about it
But as I come to terms–
It taught me,
Choices are made.
They can be made the same
Or be changed–
They are never truly set in stone,
Even when left to the past

Day 2: Thursday the 13th

2

At what point am I being too patient and kind?
To what extent do I look like a foolish pushover?
The thoughts that cover the walls of my mind–
Paint overlay wallpapered memories
And just beneath that,
Resides the brick wall

When 2+1 Gives You: Day 3

Life is starting to feel like a neverending game
of Uno
Who has the Monopoly on my time?
Every card in hand dealt
And I'm still trying to Queen up.
Tried stacking my checkers in a game of Chess
Even threw a few jacks in with the dice–
Hoping to get 7 twice.
Guess my style never changed,
Since I'm still playing 21

Day 4: Handle with Care

It is all in the heart.
(the) Life.
(the) Blood.
It is an engine.
A solar-powered battery.
How ironic that this, "thing",
Be the (baggage) handler of love, too

Day 5: Sunday Morning

Therapy sessions in the backyard.
Bugs dance around me, as birds' song grows.
Of course, the wind had to chime in.

Still Day 5...

Anymore, I do not have much to say.
So much in my mind and on my heart
But I am learning which battles are mine

For Pity's Sake: Day 6

Helpless or hopeless
I am a romantic, at best.
I have scars for days
But jokes for weeks--
Some to hide the pain
And a dash more to numb me.
Call it knee jerk
Except it is more so for the tears.
I have shed too many, in crowded rooms
Just for crickets to have their 15 minutes of
fame.
Not looking for pity, party of one.
Just a moment to be vulnerable--
I am but a helpless and hopeless romantic, after
all

Day 7: Growing

You grow.
You grow to love
And you grow to love people–
In such an inexplicable way.
You do not know how, when, where, or why it
happens
But it does and all you can do is let go

Day 8: If I Told You There Was More, Would You Believe Me

I wear my scars on my sleeves,
Covering them with cloth.
Just enough, however, for all to see–
Should they take a peek.
Reminders of who I came from
And faces I have been.
I wear my scars on my sleeves–
Reminding me of what I used to be.
The pieces I purposefully cover, unveil
themselves–
For the voyeuring, wondering, eye that is
Still unable to pinpoint the mystery I can be.
I am the canvas,
So I wear my tattoos on my sleeves–
Uncovering them in moments of vulnerability
and grandeur.
Just enough, however, for few to see.

Day 9: Life Goes On

Feeling
Shortchanged at times--
Because I lost my sense.
Or may be trying to find it all along.
Neither here nor anywhere.
All speculation
But how do I articulate
What I want to say
Without wires?
Crossed and tapped,
Recording the moments that do not matter,
Just for them to replay.
Trauma, drama, and other misnomers.
Whatever I call it,
The diagnosis points--
Like (a) needle on (a) compass--
To the choices I made in lessen.
Putting the "o(h)" in lesson--
The substantial gainful activity
That would, eventually, build me

Day 10: The Words We Do Not Speak

Looking into my eyes,
I do not see the same person.
I do not remember her,
Yet I hold her memories
And I hold them tight.
Upon release,
I realized she left something inside of me.
Don't know if it is life or death–
At times it feels more like fear.
Out of all the things I left my self,
I chose fear.
It wasn't the people she loved and knew.
She helped me with that war,
Until I could stand on my own.
She
Left
Me--
With fear.
Yet, I no longer curse her name.
I hold her fear but I still have love for her, in my heart.
A love so strong that I cannot stay mad at her.
Truth be told…
I would not have gotten to know me

If not for,
My love of her.

Day 11: In Existence

12

When I think of my mistakes
I can only chalk them up to– choices were made.
Some people, places, and things
Should have been left but I chose right.

Although the thoughts occasionally keep me up
at night–
waking up does not feel as tough.

Day 12: Punitive Jeopardy

I go through a lot that I don't speak of–
Private affairs, if you will.
I tussle with the thought:
Could this be because of my choices or is it,
"just life"?
Similar stories come from different sources
But if so many share the same experience,
Why do I feel so alone?

Day 13: The Waltz

Masquerade
In the form of daily living.
Dancing,
Exchanging partners as we go.
Turn left.
Hands up.
Now side step.
Collecting gazes in our pockets--
Saving up to feed the ego later.
Masks up,
Clenched jaws.
Wait for it...
Round of applause

Day 14: The Pros and Cons
of a Mausoleum

All I ask,
Is that my eulogy
Be delivered like a soliloquy.
Line by line,
Read my rights,
For the times I wore my wrongs.
Seeds planted in tainted soil,
Can't always reap what they sew.
If I had to be dark,
I would be knight.
Sword and armor in hand,
As I valiantly rode in on my broken down horse
and rescued myself.
All I ask, is that my eulogy
Be delivered...
Just how I lived.

Day 15: Expenditures

On the inside, looking out–
Asking to come to the out, now.
Fast forward, rewind, pause, play.
I hit "record" after the moments I fail to cherish.
Immediately judging myself, upon eject(ion).

(Thursday- July 27, 2023)

Day 16: When the Pulp is Fiction

Just as my mind goes blank,
I can feel peace coursing within
But the thoughts come charging in.
Two by two, reminders attempt execution.
I should have...
I need to...
Remember when...
Maybe...
By the fifth hit, I am weak.
Do I give in to the doubts and thoughts
Or seek refuge and heal?

Day 17: Carrying the Weight of the Word

The struggle seems real, sometimes,
But it's not a daytime job like it used to be.
24/7, 365…
366, if I was feeling lucky.
The amount of chaos I kept myself in,
Hoping to feel experiences and
To see
Words…
It was all in the name of words.
I needed to see the spoken, come to life.
Bringing me trouble but giving me peace,
This double-edged sword
Writes poetry on my heart

Day 18: Is This Thing On?

We do not always have to go toe to toe,
With that voice inside our heads.
You know, the one that says this is as good as it
gets.
What if the good could be even greater
But we accept good,
Because we think that is where it's safe?
Not even about survival
But our roots are so conditioned,
We believe it to be true.
Because "you know what they say".
Who are they
And why should anyone know what they say,
In any given circumstance?
How would they know another's feelings,
If still...we do not even know what they say?
Unless they say,
Live…
Love…
And be free…
Should we have much more to say, than they?
Or are the voices inside and out, that deafening?

Day 19: Act 1

Fade In

Close-up.

The pages are a scene and the words are actors.
Lines delivered--
Via stylograph.

Rack focus.

Unbeknownst to the audience,
The Scriptwriter is behind the scenes--
In an unfamiliar corridor,
Thrashing about–
Hoping to finish the script before the first cut.

Applause,
In round,
Could be had at idiom's end–
But head and heart never play fair.
Would it be unorthodox to write for both?
Despite indecision–
As is the forté–
The show must go on.

Fade Out

Day 20: Macro

I am in a world
Where what lives, exists.
It asks not.
Wants not.
Never questions
But simply, exists.
Steady growing and receiving,
All that is needed--
Yet we beg, steal, and borrow--
Medicating the sorrow.
I am in a world
With more information
Than ever before.
Existing among people
Who want more.
Watching true beauty
Unfold around them
And still see lack.
Where medication supersedes meditation--
A world that exists but fails at living.
I am in this world
But (am) not of it

Day 21: A Night of Wonder

Yesterday, I chased the Sun and found the Moon.
I can appreciate the light in both
But something about the Sun,
Increases my glow.
My heart yearned for a closer view.
Upon arrival, it was already hidden behind the clouds.
In my dismay, I decided to appreciate the moment--
So I carried on.
I could have gone home
But, instead, took a different route
In the wait, I found adventure and life.
As I sat with patience,
The Moon came to me--
Just to say,
It too
Spoke the language of the Sun.